Credit Card Secrets for Building Wealth & Rewards

A Step-by-Step Guide to Using Credit Cards, 0% APR, and Business Credit to Build Wealth, Earn Rewards, and Create Lasting Financial Freedom

By Joe Correa

AF849263

Published by Live Stronger Faster

Copyright © 2025 by Joe Correa

All rights reserved.

No part of this publication may be reproduced, distributed, or transmitted in any form or by any means—electronic, mechanical, photocopying, recording, or otherwise—without the prior written permission of the publisher, except in the case of brief quotations embodied in critical reviews and certain other noncommercial uses permitted by copyright law.

This book is for educational and informational purposes only. The author and publisher are not engaged in rendering legal, financial, or other professional advice. Readers should consult a qualified professional before making any financial decisions.

First Edition

TABLE OF CONTENTS

Introduction: The Flight That Changed Everything

I never intended to become a credit card expert. In fact, the first time I was offered a credit card in college, I only signed up because they were giving away a free T-shirt. It was red, too big, and had the bank's logo splashed across the front. That shirt cost me almost $3,000 in debt over the next year. That was my introduction to the credit trap—not the wealth-building machine I know today.

Years later, I found myself sitting in the back of a coach flight, knees crushed, dreading the 5-hour trip ahead. Across the aisle sat a man, maybe in his early 40s, sipping champagne in first class. I couldn't help but wonder how some people seem to live in a completely different financial world.

When we landed, I noticed him at the baggage carousel, rolling a sleek carry-on with the American Express Platinum tag hanging from the handle. As we exited, I worked up the courage to say, "Excuse me, can I ask... how do you travel like that?"

He smiled and said something that stuck with me forever:

"It's not money. It's points. I haven't paid for a flight in five years."

That moment triggered an obsession. I dove into everything I could about credit cards, rewards systems, point transfers, 0% APR strategies, and how the wealthy use credit as a *tool,* not a trap. I devoured forums, YouTube videos, and financial blogs.

I tested every strategy. I failed, got rejected, had my credit limit slashed. But slowly, I started winning.

I discovered the real power wasn't just in earning free flights—it was in unlocking capital, funding businesses, stacking credit limits, and converting rewards into cash flow. Most importantly, I learned how to avoid the traps that most people fall into—those hidden fees, interest spikes, and false promises.

One of the biggest shifts happened when I used a 0% interest card to buy inventory for a side business that turned into a six-figure brand. Another time, I earned over $1,200 in sign-up bonuses within a month by timing my applications and expenses just right.

The deeper I went, the clearer it became: Credit cards weren't the enemy. **They were a gateway to financial leverage**, lifestyle upgrades, and even generational wealth—**if** used strategically.

This book isn't just about getting points or avoiding debt. It's about unlocking the systems that banks use to make billions—and flipping them to work for *you*. Whether you want to travel the world for free, launch a business, or just get control over your finances, this book is your starting point.

You're about to learn the secrets the banks *hope* you never discover.

Welcome to *Credit Card Secrets for Building Wealth & Rewards*.
Let's change the way you use credit—forever.

Chapter 1: Understanding the Credit Card System — How Banks Profit and How You Can Flip the Script

"If you don't understand how the system works, you become a victim of it."
— Joe Correa

The True Purpose of a Credit Card

Most people believe credit cards are just a convenience—something to keep in your wallet for emergencies, travel, or impulse purchases. But to banks, credit cards are far more than that. They are **highly profitable financial products** designed to earn money in multiple ways:

- **Interest on carried balances**
- **Annual fees**
- **Late fees and penalties**
- **Interchange fees paid by merchants**
- **Balance transfer fees**
- **Cash advance fees**

Banks are not in the business of giving you credit because they're kind—they do it because **the average American pays hundreds of dollars in interest and fees every year.**

But here's the secret: **You can use the system without falling into the trap.**

The moment you understand the blueprint, you can:

✓ Access capital at 0% interest

✓ Earn thousands in points and cashback

✓ Travel for free

✓ Launch side businesses

✓ Build a 750+ credit score and leverage it for even more wealth

Types of Credit Cards and Their Purposes

There are **five primary types of credit cards** you should be familiar with:

1. **Cashback Cards**
Ideal for everyday spending. Look for:

☐ Flat-rate cashback (e.g., 2% on all purchases)

☐ Rotating categories (e.g., 5% on groceries, gas, etc.)

2. **Travel Rewards Cards**
Best for earning airline miles or hotel points. Key features:

☐ Sign-up bonuses (50,000–100,000 points)

☐ Transfer partners for maximum value

☐ Perks like lounge access and free checked bags

3. **Balance Transfer Cards**
Designed for debt management.

☐ Offer 0% APR for 12–21 months

☐ Ideal for consolidating or eliminating high-interest debt

4. **Business Credit Cards**
Great for side hustles or full businesses.

☐ Higher limits

☐ Track spending by category

☐ Business-specific perks like shipping discounts or office supplies

5. **Credit Building or Secured Cards**
For those with no or poor credit.

☐ Requires a deposit

☐ Reports to all three bureaus

☐ Helps you establish or rebuild your credit profile

Tip: You should never apply randomly. Each card has a purpose, and your selection should match your **financial goals**.

How Credit Card Companies Make Money (and How to Make It Back)

Banks make money in **three main ways**:

1. **Revolving Interest**

The majority of cardholders carry a balance. At an average APR of 20%, the interest compounds fast.
Strategy: Never carry a balance. Pay in full every month.

2. **Merchant Fees**

Every time you swipe, the merchant pays 1.5–3.5% to the card network. That's why cards with rewards are possible.
Strategy: Maximize your return by using the right card for every purchase.

3. **Annual and Penalty Fees**

Annual fees can be worth it—but only if you **use the perks**. Late fees, on the other hand, are to be avoided at all costs.
Strategy: Automate payments and track due dates.

Tools You Need Before Playing the Game

Before you dive in, set up your financial toolset:

1. **Credit Monitoring** – Use platforms like Credit Karma or MyFICO.

2. **Budget Tracker** – Mint, YNAB, or a simple spreadsheet.

3. **Card Benefits Organizer** – Create a table or use an app to track your cards' rewards, due dates, and perks.

4. **Payment Automation** – Always automate at least the minimum payment to avoid late fees.

5. **Spending Goals** – Only use cards for **planned, budgeted expenses**.

Think of your credit card strategy as a business plan. You're not spending emotionally—you're **earning strategically**.

Mindset Shift – From Consumer to Wealth Builder

Here's the most important concept of this chapter:

Credit cards are not for spending money you don't have. They are for **earning rewards on money you're already going to spend.**

This one shift can be life-changing.

For example:

- If you spend $2,000/month on bills, food, gas, and groceries, that's $24,000/year.

- At 2% cashback, that's $480 back in your pocket—without changing your lifestyle.

- With travel cards, it could mean **2–3 roundtrip flights every year.**

- Use multiple cards smartly, and you can earn **over $1,500 in rewards or bonuses** yearly with minimal effort.

And when paired with 0% interest promotions, you can **borrow money for free** and invest it into cash-flowing ventures (covered in later chapters).

ACTION STEPS FOR CHAPTER 1:

1. List your current credit cards and categorize them.

2. Identify which ones have annual fees and which rewards you actually use.

3. Set up auto-pay for all credit card minimums today.

4. Download a credit monitoring tool and track your score.

5. Create a spreadsheet with your card names, due dates, limits, and reward structures.

This is the foundation. In the next chapter, you'll learn **how to apply for new credit cards like a pro**, time your applications, maximize your approval odds, and unlock the **best welcome bonuses** banks offer.

Are you ready to start stacking rewards instead of debt? Let's go.

Marco's story

Marcos always paid with cash. In his mind, credit cards were trouble. He had seen his parents go through it—minimum payments, sleepless nights, collection calls. So when he turned 25 and landed his first steady job in sales, he stuck to the basics: debit card, cash, and a promise to never borrow money.

Every morning, he stopped by his favorite Miami coffee shop before work. The barista, Nikki, would greet him with the same question: “Café con leche, Marcos?” He’d smile, hand over a $5 bill, and head out the door. But one morning, something odd happened. The man in front of him ordered the same drink and scanned a shiny black credit card. The barista handed him a loyalty punch card, and the man nodded, “Put it on the Sapphire. Double points this month.”

Marcos tilted his head. Double points?

He watched as the man walked away, sipping his coffee with a confidence that intrigued him. Marcos asked, “What’s the deal with that card?”

The barista shrugged. “He’s always talking about points. Says he flew to Greece for free last year.”

Free? The word echoed in Marcos’ head for days.

Later that week, curiosity got the best of him. He went home, opened his laptop, and typed in, “How do credit card points work?” That innocent search led to an all-night rabbit hole—articles, YouTube videos, blog posts. He learned about welcome bonuses, travel hacking, cashback, and 0% APR promotions.

That weekend, he applied for his first real credit card: a no-annual-fee cashback card offering $200 for spending $500 in three months. Simple enough. He figured he could use it for gas and groceries and pay it off immediately.

A month later, he had the $200 bonus in his account and had spent nothing extra to earn it.

That was the beginning.

At work, he started using cards for all reimbursable business travel. He opened a spreadsheet to track due dates, rewards, and limits. Over the next six months, he added a travel card with a 60,000-point bonus and a business card for his side hustle selling custom t-shirts online.

Every purchase became intentional. He stopped seeing credit as temptation and started seeing it as a strategy. His credit score shot from 688 to 742 in less than a year. He used a 0% APR card to buy new printing equipment for his t-shirt business and doubled his sales that quarter.

By year two, Marcos had earned over $3,500 in rewards, taken two trips using points, and never paid a cent in interest.

But the real transformation came one night in December.

His cousin Daniela called him in tears. Her car had broken down, and she didn't have enough for repairs. She had bad credit, no savings, and couldn't get approved for a loan. Without the car, she'd lose her job. Marcos didn't hesitate. He used his 0% card to cover the cost and set up a payment plan with her.

"Why are you helping me like this?" she asked.

"Because I've been learning how to use the system. And now I finally feel like I'm in control."

That Christmas, Marcos flew his parents to New York for the first time in their lives using points. He covered the hotel stay with his card's travel portal and earned another 10,000 points on the spend. His dad, a quiet man with rough hands from years of construction work, leaned over and said, "I never thought this kind of life was possible for us."

"It is," Marcos replied. "If we stop fearing credit—and start using it smart."

The coffee shop where it all started still stood on the corner. But Marcos had changed. Now he ordered his drink with his favorite rewards card, and Nikki would say, "Still stacking points, huh?"

Always, he'd say with a grin.

Because for Marcos, credit wasn't just a tool—it was a second chance, a passport, and a wealth strategy.

And it all started with curiosity and a cup of coffee.

Chapter 2: The Smart Application Strategy – Getting Approved, Maximizing Bonuses, and Timing It Right

"The difference between being denied and being rewarded thousands is all in the timing and the strategy."
— Joe Correa

Why You Shouldn't Apply Randomly

Most people apply for credit cards without a plan. They see a flashy commercial, an influencer post, or a preapproval letter in the mail—and they click apply.

That's a mistake.

Every application results in a hard inquiry on your credit report, which temporarily lowers your credit score by 2 to 5 points. More importantly, too many inquiries in a short period raise red flags to lenders.

But when you apply strategically, you:

✓ Maximize approval odds

✓ Earn the highest welcome bonuses

✓ Increase your total available credit

✓ Build your credit score faster

Timing is everything. And so is knowing which cards to apply for, in what order, and why.

The Approval Formula (Yes, there is a formula!)

To get approved for top-tier credit cards, you need to understand what lenders are looking for. Here are the **five key factors** they analyze:

1. **Credit Score (FICO):**

680+ for mid-tier cards

720+ for premium cards

Scores below 650 will likely require secured or starter cards

2. **Credit History:**

Lenders prefer 2+ years of credit history

No recent delinquencies, collections, or charge-offs

3. **Credit Utilization:**

Keep usage under 30%, ideally under 10%

Example: $1,000 balance on $10,000 limit = 10%

4. **Number of Recent Inquiries:**

0–2 in the past 6 months = strong

4+ = considered risky or "credit hungry"

5. **Total Accounts and Mix:**

A mix of revolving credit (cards) and installment loans (car, mortgage, student loan) helps

Having 3–5 open cards shows experience without being risky

Pro Tip: If your credit isn't quite where it needs to be, focus on increasing your score for 60–90 days before applying. You can do this by lowering utilization, disputing errors, and becoming an authorized user on a high-limit, low-balance card.

The Application Plan — 3 Types of Cards to Target

Before applying, decide what your goal is:

1. **Welcome Bonus Cash or Points**

☑ Ideal for funding a vacation, building emergency funds, or launching a side business

☑ Look for cards offering $200–$750 after spending $500–$4,000 in 3 months

2. **0% APR Offers**

☑ Perfect for big purchases or debt payoff

☑ Many cards offer 0% APR for 12–21 months on purchases or balance transfers

3. **Business Credit Cards**

☑ Higher limits, don't appear on personal report, and offer massive sign-up bonuses

☑ Even side hustles like freelancing or reselling qualify

Rule of Thumb:

- Apply for **personal cards first**, then **business cards**
- Apply for cards from **different banks**, not all from the same issuer
- Space out applications by **at least 90 days**, unless you're executing a stacking strategy (covered in Chapter 6)

Bank Application Rules You Must Know

Each bank has its own internal rules. Violating them often leads to automatic denial, even if you have great credit.

Here are the most important:

Chase 5/24 Rule

- If you've opened **5 or more credit cards** (personal only) in the past 24 months from **any bank**, you will be denied most Chase cards
- Apply for Chase cards **first** in your strategy

Amex "Once Per Lifetime" Rule

- You can only earn the **welcome bonus** for each card **once per lifetime**

- Wait until you can meet the minimum spend before applying

Citi 8/65/95 Rule

- You can only apply for **1 personal Citi card every 8 days** and **2 every 65 days**

Bank of America 2/3/4 Rule

- No more than **2 cards in 2 months**, **3 in 12 months**, and **4 in 24 months**

Knowing these rules helps you avoid denials and wasted hard inquiries.

How to Meet Minimum Spend Without Overspending

Many cards require you to spend $500–$5,000 in 90 days to earn the welcome bonus. But don't panic or overspend—use these strategies:

- **Prepay utilities or insurance** (monthly bills you're paying anyway)

- **Buy gift cards** to places you shop regularly (groceries gas, Amazon)

- **Pay rent with a service like Plastiq** (with smal fees—still worth it for large bonuses)

- **Split large purchases with family/friends and get reimbursed**

- **Use the card for all business or reimbursable work expenses**

Warning: Don't just spend to hit the bonus if you can't pay it off. Remember: the interest is never worth the rewards.

ACTION STEPS FOR CHAPTER 2:

1. **Check your credit report** and score on Credit Karma, Experian, or MyFICO.

2. **Identify your next 1–2 card goals**: cashback, travel, 0% APR, or business.

3. **Choose a card that matches your goal** and current credit profile.

4. **Review the bank's rules** before applying (especially if it's Chase).

5. **Plan how you'll meet the minimum spend** using budgeted, regular expenses.

6. **Apply and track your cards in a spreadsheet** with due dates, bonuses, limits, and category rewards.

Let's talk about Alicia and her journey.

It was a Wednesday evening, and Alicia sat at her tiny kitchen table in a cramped apartment just outside Atlanta, staring at her laptop. On the screen was a Chase Sapphire Preferred card application. Her heart was racing. She'd filled out all the fields, read the bonus offer three times—**60,000 points after spending $4,000 in three months**—but she couldn't bring herself to click "submit."

Her finger hovered over the mouse.

She took a breath and closed the browser.

It wasn't the first time.

Alicia had grown up in a family that feared credit. Her mother called credit cards "debt traps" and warned her never to get one. So for most of her twenties, Alicia operated on cash and a debit card. No credit history, no debt—but also, no opportunities.

Then came the promotion at work. She had just stepped into a marketing manager role and was now traveling for conferences, meeting with vendors, and managing budgets. Her boss used a company credit card. Alicia, however, fronted her travel costs and waited to be reimbursed.

On her first trip to San Diego, she overheard a coworker talking about redeeming points for a five-star hotel stay. Alicia was floored. She had stayed in a basic motel that reeked of mildew just to save money. Her coworker had used points—**earned from spending she already had to do**—and was enjoying oceanfront luxury. That night, Alicia went down the credit rabbit hole.

By the time she was back home, she knew about welcome bonuses, 0% interest periods, and bank approval rules. She signed up for Credit Karma and discovered her score was 712—not bad for someone who'd never had a real credit card.

So why the hesitation?

It was fear. Fear of doing it wrong. Fear of rejection. Fear of debt.

She started small. A week later, she applied for a simple cashback card with a $200 bonus after spending $500. Approved. She used it for groceries, gas, and her Netflix bill. She paid it off every Friday. After three months, her score had jumped to 730. Confidence built.

That's when she pulled the Chase Sapphire back up again. This time, she wasn't nervous. She'd checked her 5/24 status—only one new card in the past 24 months. She'd timed it perfectly. She even wrote out a plan to meet the $4,000 spend: her next flight and hotel, new tires for her car, and helping her sister with a medical bill. All expenses she had already planned—now working toward her goal.

She clicked "Submit."

Approved instantly. $20,000 credit limit.

Her jaw dropped.

That same month, Alicia took another leap—she opened a business credit card under her Etsy side hustle, which she ran on nights and weekends. It sold custom mugs and printables. She'd made only a few hundred dollars a month so far, but now she had a real business checking account and a business credit card. That one came with a $500 bonus after spending $3,000.

Her strategy became airtight:

- Business expenses on the business card

- Personal and travel costs on the Sapphire

- Spreadsheet tracking rewards, due dates, and payment status

- Automation to pay minimums, manual payments every week

In 60 days, she had collected **over $800 in bonuses**, was approved for $35,000 total credit, and still hadn't paid a penny in interest.

Three months later, Alicia stood barefoot on a balcony in Maui, sipping pineapple juice and watching the sunrise. The trip had cost her less than $200 out of pocket. Everything else—flight, hotel, rental car—was covered in points.

She snapped a picture and posted it online. The caption read:
"Debt-free, paid in points, and stress-free. This is how you use credit."

Messages poured in: "How did you do that?" "Teach me!" "What's the trick?"

But there wasn't a trick. It was a strategy. And it had changed everything.

From fear to freedom, Alicia had learned that credit wasn't the enemy.

The enemy was not knowing how to use it.

Chapter 3: Maximizing Credit Card Rewards – Travel, Cashback, and Hidden Perks

"Earning points is just the beginning. The real wealth is in knowing how to use them."
— Unknown

The Three Types of Credit Card Rewards

When used properly, credit cards offer significant rewards that go far beyond cashback. These rewards come in three primary forms:

1. **Cashback**

Flat-rate or tiered percentages back on your purchases

Best for simple, flexible usage

Ideal for people who want real cash without the complexity of points

2. Points

Often part of a bank's reward ecosystem (e.g., Chase Ultimate Rewards, Amex Membership Rewards)

Redeemable for travel, gift cards, cash, or transferred to travel partners

Offer the highest potential value when used correctly

3. Miles

Airline-specific or flexible miles systems

Great for frequent travelers

Can yield 1.5x to 5x the value of cashback if optimized for premium travel

Quick Comparison:

✓ Cashback = simplicity

✓ Points = flexibility

✓ Miles = maximum travel value

How to Use Points for Free Travel

The average user redeems points for gift cards or statement credits—usually at a value of $0.01 per point. But smart users get **2–5x more** by transferring points to **travel partners**.

Example:

Chase Sapphire Preferred users can transfer points to programs like:

- United Airlines
- Hyatt Hotels
- British Airways
- JetBlue

So instead of redeeming 50,000 points for $500 in gift cards, you might get:

- A roundtrip flight to Europe worth $1,000+

- 3 nights at a luxury Hyatt resort worth $1,500

Redemption Tools:

- **Google Flights**: To find the cash cost of flights
- **AwardHacker.com**: To compare point values across loyalty programs
- **Transfer partners chart** (available from your card issuer's website)

Rule of Thumb: Transfer only when you're ready to book. Once transferred, points can't be reversed.

Cashback Maximization Strategies

Cashback may seem basic, but there are advanced ways to maximize it:

1. **Use Multiple Cards Strategically**

One card for gas, another for groceries, and a third for everything else

Example: Use the **Citi Custom Cash** for 5% back on your top spending category

2. **Stack Rewards with Portals and Apps**

Shop through **Rakuten**, **Honey**, or your card's own portal to earn extra

Some portals offer 10–20% back on specific brands

3. **Redeem for Statement Credits or Bank Deposits**

Avoid redeeming for merchandise or gift cards unless it gives 1:1 value or better

4. **Avoid Annual Fee Cards Unless Perks Exceed Cost**

Do the math: If a $95 card earns you $400/year in cashback, it's worth it. If not, downgrade or switch.

Hidden Perks Most Cardholders Miss

Most people never use the full value of their cards. Here are **high-value benefits** to look out for:

- **Cell Phone Insurance**

Use a card like Wells Fargo Active Cash to pay your cell bill, and get up to $600 in protection.

- **Extended Warranty & Purchase Protection**

Many cards extend warranties by an extra year or protect against theft or damage within 90–120 days.

- **Trip Delay & Cancellation Coverage**

Premium travel cards offer reimbursement if your trip is delayed, cancelled, or interrupted.

- **Lounge Access**

Cards like the Amex Platinum or Capital One Venture X offer access to airport lounges with food, drinks, and Wi-Fi.

- **Global Entry / TSA PreCheck Credits**

Many travel cards reimburse the $85–$100 application fee every 4–5 years.

- **Hotel Status**

Some cards give you instant elite hotel status, which includes free upgrades, breakfast, and late checkout.

Pro Tip: Call your card's benefits line once you're approved and ask for a list of all included perks. They often provide PDFs or online dashboards.

The Rule of ROI — Return on Intent

Before chasing rewards, always ask:

"Am I using this card to earn something on spending I already planned, or am I spending more to chase perks?"

Rewards only work if you:

- Stay within your monthly budget
- Pay the balance in full each month
- Don't fall for marketing that encourages overspending

A $200 cashback reward is not a win if you pay $300 in interest.

The wealth is in the strategy.

ACTION STEPS FOR CHAPTER 3:

1. List all current credit cards and their rewards programs.
2. Organize them into: Cashback, Points, or Miles.
3. Visit your card's reward portal and review transfer partners or cash redemption options.
4. Set a reward goal: Is it travel, cashback savings, or a major purchase?

5. Use a spreadsheet or app (like AwardWallet) to track your rewards and perks.

6. Evaluate each card's annual fee against real benefits used. If the ROI is low, plan to downgrade or switch.

"The Honeymoon That Points Paid For"

Samantha and Jordan had just gotten engaged. She was a school teacher. He was a firefighter. Their dream honeymoon was a two-week trip to Italy—Rome, Florence, and a relaxing finale on the Amalfi Coast. But the price tag was brutal: over $6,500 just for flights and hotels.

"No way we can afford that," Jordan sighed as they scrolled through a travel site at midnight, sitting on their secondhand couch. "We'll just do something local. Maybe a beach weekend."

But Samantha wasn't ready to let go of the dream.

The next morning, while sipping her coffee before work, she remembered something her older sister had mentioned months earlier: "You know, people travel the world for free using credit card points." At the time, it sounded like a scam. But now? It was worth looking into.

She Googled: "How to use credit card points to travel for free."

That search changed everything.

By the time she got home from school, Samantha had a whole notepad filled with terms like “Chase Ultimate Rewards,” “airline transfer partners,” and “welcome bonuses.” She discovered that people were traveling first class for less than what she paid in monthly bills—all because they understood how to **maximize** the credit card game.

That night, she presented her plan to Jordan like a school project.

“Okay, hear me out,” she said, flipping open her notepad. “We can get the Chase Sapphire Preferred card. If we each get one, we’ll get 120,000 points. That’s enough for roundtrip flights to Rome and two nights in a hotel.”

Jordan blinked. “Wait. Just for using the card?”

“Well, yes and no. We have to spend $4,000 each in 3 months. But here’s how we’ll do it: we’ll pay all our bills with the card, buy gift cards for groceries and gas, and I already talked to your brother about helping with the down payment for his wedding venue. We put it on the card, he pays us back.”

He stared at her. “You’re serious about this.”

“I’m 100% serious,” she said. “We can turn everyday spending into this trip. No debt. No interest. Just strategy.”

Three months later, it was working.

Between welcome bonuses, referral points, and cashing in rewards, Samantha had booked two roundtrip flights to Rome for $89 in taxes. She used the Sapphire travel portal to book a boutique hotel in Florence, paying with points. Then, she transferred points to Hyatt for three nights on the Amalfi Coast in a cliffside suite that would've cost over $1,200.

"I feel like a travel hacker," she whispered to herself while confirming the last booking.

They didn't stop there. Samantha signed up for Rakuten and linked it to her card. Every time she shopped for wedding items online, she earned 3%–10% back on top of her card rewards. Jordan used his business credit card for gear and supplies for his woodworking side hustle. More points. More cash back.

By the time the wedding arrived, they had covered:

- All flights with points
- 6 of the 10 hotel nights using transferred miles
- Rental car and excursions with cashback rewards
- Even the luggage, which was bought with a card perk covering 90-day purchase protection

Italy was everything they had dreamed of—and more.

They ate pasta under a canopy of stars in Trastevere, watched the sun set over Ponte Vecchio, and drank espresso on a private balcony facing the Mediterranean. Every moment felt like luxury. And the best part?

They paid **less than $300 total** for the entire trip.

Jordan looked at Samantha while they waited to board their flight home. "You just saved us six grand," he said. "You're like a travel wizard."

She smiled. "Nope. Just someone who read the fine print and followed the rules."

Back home, they didn't stop. They created a spreadsheet, labeled every card they had, tracked benefits, and set reward goals for their next trip—Japan in the spring. Jordan even shared the story with the guys at the fire station, and three of them signed up for cards that week.

Samantha started a little blog on the side: *Travel Like a Teacher*. Within months, she had an audience, affiliate links bringing in passive income, and emails pouring in from people asking, "Can you show me how you did it?"

She always replied the same way:
"Yes. Start by using the money you already spend—and learn the system the banks use to keep us broke."

In less than a year, Samantha and Jordan turned a dream honeymoon into a lifestyle. Not because they made more money—but because they **used their money smarter**.

The rewards were never just about points. They were about freedom, options, and knowing how to make every dollar work harder.

And it all started with a notepad, a cup of coffee, and the courage to click "Apply."

Chapter 4: Building Massive Credit Limits and Leveraging 0% APR for Strategic Growth

"Credit is not just a score. It's a source of capital—and a smart person's bank."
— Joe Correa

Why You Need Higher Credit Limits

The average American has a credit card limit of around $5,000—but people who understand how to build and leverage credit can access **$50,000–$150,000+ in available credit** across personal and business cards.

Here's why higher limits matter:

✓ **Lower utilization = higher credit scores**

✓ **Access to 0% interest capital for large purchases or investments**

✓ **More rewards from higher spending capacity**

✓ **Increased financial flexibility during emergencies**

Think of your credit limit as a **cash reserve** you don't need until you do. The more you have, the less you stress.

How to Increase Your Credit Limits (Without Hurting Your Score)

Here's how to build large credit limits the smart way:

Step 1: Start with your current cards

- Use your card consistently for 3–6 months

- Pay off in full every month (or keep utilization under 10%)

- Request a **credit limit increase online** or call customer service

Pro Tip:
Use phrases like, "I've been using this card for regular expenses and would like a limit increase to support larger purchases and improve my utilization."

Most banks allow **soft pull** requests, meaning no impact to your score.

Step 2: Apply for additional cards strategically

- Space out new applications (every 3–4 months)

- Target banks with generous limits (Amex, Chase, Capital One, Navy Federal Credit Union)

- Consider **business credit cards**, which often offer higher starting limits

Step 3: Combine limits (if allowed)

Some banks, like Chase and Bank of America, allow you to **reallocate credit** between cards. If one card has $10,000 and another has $2,000, you may be able to move $5,000 over—creating higher limits where you need them most.

Step 4: Show income growth

If your income has increased, update it in your credit profile. This often qualifies you for higher limits—even if your score hasn't changed much.

Reminder:
Banks don't verify income unless it's unusually high or you're applying for large loans. Be honest, but know that **your reported income influences your credit limits.**

Using 0% APR Offers Like a Financial Tool

One of the **most powerful advantages** of credit cards is **0% interest introductory periods**, usually lasting **12 to 21 months**. That's up to **1.5 years of free capital**—if you know how to use it.

What You Can Use 0% APR For:

☑ Launching a side hustle or small business

☑ Paying off high-interest debt (via balance transfer)

☑ Buying inventory or equipment to generate income

☑Covering short-term emergencies without interest penalties

☑ Pre-paying large expenses like insurance, tuition, or property taxes

Caution:
Only use 0% APR offers for **planned, profitable, or essential purposes**. Not for lifestyle upgrades or emotional purchases.

How to Use 0% APR Effectively:

1. **Create a plan** for how the funds will be used and repaid

2. **Set a monthly repayment goal** (e.g., divide total borrowed by number of 0% months)

3. **Avoid adding new charges** to the same card—some issuers apply payments to older balances first

4. **Track the expiration date** of the promotional period to avoid high-interest surprises

Example:
You open a card with a 15-month 0% APR on purchases. You use $4,500 to launch an online course business. You plan to pay $300/month for 15 months. If the business earns $1,000/month, you've used bank money to create leverage—with no interest paid.

Managing Large Limits Without Debt Risk

Getting access to $100,000 in available credit doesn't mean you should use all of it. The **golden rule** of responsible credit use remains:

Only spend what you can pay off—ideally within 30 days.

To stay in control:

- Set up **weekly balance alerts** on each card
- Use **autopay** to avoid missed payments
- Review statements monthly to catch errors or overspending
- Use cards for **planned expenses** only, not lifestyle inflation

Remember: Credit is leverage. Not income.

Tracking and Managing It All

As your credit access grows, you need systems to stay organized:

Use tools like:

✔ **Credit Karma or MyFICO** to monitor score changes

✔ **Spreadsheets** to track card names, limits, due dates, APR periods, rewards

✔ **Personal finance apps** like Mint or Monarch Money to manage spending and payments

✔ **AwardWallet or Travel Freely** to track card perks, travel credits, and expiration dates

ACTION STEPS FOR CHAPTER 4:

1. List all current cards and their credit limits.

2. Request a credit limit increase on 1–2 cards this week.

3. Identify a 0% APR offer you could use for a profitable or essential purchase.

4. Create a payoff plan to use that credit **strategically**, not emotionally.

5. Set up a spreadsheet or app to track your total available credit, usage, and limits.

6. Begin preparing for your next card application by cleaning up your credit report and ensuring your income data is accurate.

"From Broke to Builder: How Malik Used Credit to Launch His Dream"

Malik was tired of watching others win while he barely kept up.

He had a good job—IT support for a hospital network—but it was just that... good. It paid the bills, left little to save, and no room to take risks. And Malik was ready to build *something*. Something of his own.

He'd always dreamed of launching an online tech coaching service—helping everyday people fix computers, set up smart homes, or recover lost files. He already helped neighbors and family members on weekends, for free or fifty bucks here and there.

But to launch it online, he needed equipment—new lighting, a backdrop, a better mic, screen-capture software, a website. Total cost? About $3,200. Malik had $380 in his savings account.

Then, one night while watching YouTube, he stumbled across a video titled:
"How I Used 0% APR Credit Cards to Build My Business."
He clicked.

That video opened a door.

He learned about **introductory 0% APR offers**—credit cards that let you borrow money for 12 to 21 months interest-free. He learned that if he had good credit, he could get approved for $5,000, maybe even $10,000. And if he used that money wisely, he could build something before the promo ended—and never pay a penny in interest.

It didn't feel like debt. It felt like a bridge.

Malik checked his credit score: 738. Solid.

The next day, he applied for the **Chase Freedom Unlimited** card. He was approved instantly—**$10,000 limit and 0% APR for 15 months.** His heart raced. It felt like someone had just handed him a chance he never had before.

Within a week, he ordered everything on his list. He used $2,800 of the available credit and spent every evening building out his coaching website. On weekends, he recorded his first screen-share tutorials: "How to Speed Up a Slow Computer," "Best Free Antivirus Tools," "How to Backup Your Photos to the Cloud."

He wasn't spending recklessly. Every purchase had a purpose. Every dollar borrowed had a job.

He also made a plan: $300 per month, automatically transferred to the card, starting that month. Fifteen months to pay it off completely, interest-free.

By month four, his YouTube channel had 600 subscribers. A local real estate agent hired him to install smart home systems in three rental properties. He made $1,100 in a single weekend.

And the card? He had already paid down $1,200 of the balance—**with business income.**

One day, while logging into his credit dashboard, Malik noticed something new. An offer from American Express: a **business card with a $250 bonus, 0% APR, and no personal credit impact** if pre-qualified.

He applied. Approved again—this time for $15,000.

That's when it hit him.

He now had access to over $25,000 in credit, all because he used it the right way.

No overspending. No interest. Just leverage.

Malik was no longer just an employee. He was a business owner. A content creator. A tech coach.

And it all started with the courage to trust himself—and a card with 0% interest.

But the turning point came the following spring.

His friend Jamal, who owned a local clothing brand, asked how he had funded all this. "Man, I thought you had a big savings stash or something."

"Nope," Malik said, pulling out his phone. "It started right here. 0% APR. I had a plan. I tracked every dollar. I built what I needed without waiting ten years to save up."

Jamal stared at him. "You didn't go into debt?"

"No," Malik replied. "I went into **discipline.** I used the system without letting it use me."

Today, Malik runs a profitable online business. He has five cards—all paid in full—and over $60,000 in total credit access. He teaches others how to launch tech side hustles and helps his community stay away from predatory loans and high-interest traps.

Because he knows what they don't tell you in school:

Credit isn't just about scores or debt—it's **a launchpad**. If you use it right, it becomes the tool that funds your dreams.

And it all started with one yes.

Chapter 5: Using Credit Cards to Fund Profitable Side Hustles and Income Streams

"Smart credit use isn't about spending—it's about investing."
— Unknown

Credit as Capital, Not Consumption

Most people use credit cards for **spending**—vacations, restaurants, shopping. Wealth builders use credit cards for **funding**—starting a business, building assets, or creating passive income.

What if your next credit card wasn't for buying things you want—but for building the life you want?

Here's the mindset shift:

Don't use credit cards to buy liabilities.
Use them to build **income-producing assets**.

If you're approved for a $5,000–$20,000 credit limit with 0% APR for 12–18 months, you've just been handed **interest-free capital**. That's more powerful than most small business loans—and it's easier and faster to get.

The Best Low-Cost, High-ROI Side Hustles to Launch with Credit

You don't need tens of thousands of dollars to start a business. Here are some of the best ways to turn credit into profit with **low upfront costs** and high scalability:

1. Print-on-Demand E-Commerce (e.g., T-shirts, mugs, journals)

✓ Start-up cost: $300–$1,000

✓ Use credit for: Shopify subscription, design tools, samples, ad budget

✓ ROI: Easily 4x–10x per sale after platform and ad costs

2. Digital Courses or Coaching

✓ Start-up cost: $500–$1,500

✓ Use credit for: Camera, mic, online platform fees, software, ads

✓ ROI: Passive income potential, no inventory required

3. Service-Based Freelancing

✓ Start-up cost: $100–$1,000

✓ Use credit for: Website, branding, scheduling tools LinkedIn Ads

✓ ROI: High income potential—especially for tech, writing marketing, or tutoring

4. Short-Term Rentals or Airbnb Co-Hosting

✓ Start-up cost: $1,000–$3,000

✓ Use credit for: Furnishings, cleaning supplies, listing setup

✓ ROI: Monthly recurring revenue after a few bookings

5. Content Creation or YouTube Channel

✓ Start-up cost: $300–$1,500

✓ Use credit for: Camera gear, editing software, thumbnails promotion

✓ ROI: Long-term growth via monetization, affiliate links, sponsorships

All of these can be funded with a **credit card limit of $1,000–$5,000**, especially if you plan strategically and spend only on essentials.

How to Turn Credit into Cash Flow

Here's how to use a credit card as an **income generation engine** instead of a debt trap:

Step 1: Choose the Right Card

- 0% APR on purchases for at least 12 months
- No annual fee if possible
- Offers a sign-up bonus you can meet with business expenses

Step 2: Create a Budgeted Launch Plan

- Use the card only for launch-related costs
- Avoid subscriptions or recurring expenses unless essential
- Track every dollar and assign it to a specific business purpose

Step 3: Launch and Monetize Fast

- Your goal: earn income **before** the 0% APR window ends

- Start small: One product, one service, one offer

- Reinvest profits back into growth while paying down the card monthly

Step 4: Pay it Back with Profits

- Divide your total spend by the number of 0% months

- Stick to a strict repayment schedule—even if it means delaying personal spending

Example:
If you use $3,600 at 0% interest for 12 months, commit to repaying $300/month.
If your business earns $500/month, you're growing and repaying at the same time.

Red Flags and Risk Prevention

While this is a powerful strategy, here's what to **avoid**:

Using credit with no plan or business model
Don't borrow if you don't know how you'll earn it back.

Overestimating your income potential
Start lean. Test your idea before investing more.

Missing minimum payments
Set auto-pay for at least the minimum payment. One late payment can void your 0% offer.

Mixing personal and business expenses
Open a separate business checking account and keep records.

Letting lifestyle creep in
This credit is for *growth*, not personal upgrades.

When used right, **credit = control**. Used carelessly, **credit = chaos**.

Action Plan to Fund Your Side Hustle With Credit

Here's a 7-step action plan to execute this chapter's strategy:

1. **Choose your hustle:** Pick one income stream from the list above that fits your skillset.

2. **Map out expenses:** Identify startup costs and what you'll spend using the credit card.

3. **Find your 0% APR card:** Apply only after reviewing credit score, income, and current inquiries.

4. **Create a repayment plan:** Divide your spend by the number of months and commit.

5. **Launch fast and lean:** Use only what you need, focus on speed and simplicity.

6. **Track income and ROI:** Use a spreadsheet to monitor card balance, earnings, and breakeven point.

7. **Celebrate and repeat:** Once repaid, you'll have experience and proof—now scale it.

Final Thought:

"You're already spending money. What if that same money built a business instead?"

Credit isn't evil. It's neutral. It becomes **dangerous or powerful based on how you use it**.

And when used for income—not consumption—it becomes the **fuel for your financial independence**.

"The Etsy Empire That Started with a Credit Card"

Nina never saw herself as an entrepreneur. She was a preschool teacher in Denver—organized, soft-spoken, and endlessly patient. But after long days wrangling toddlers, she found peace in something unexpected: designing handmade planners and printable checklists.

Her creations—bright, floral, and neatly structured—weren't just cute. They helped her stay sane. Each time she posted her designs on Pinterest, a few followers would message her: "Where can I buy this?" She'd smile and reply, "It's just something I made for myself."

But one winter afternoon, while sipping peppermint tea and scrolling through TikTok, she stumbled across a video titled:
"I Made $7,000 Selling Printables on Etsy. Here's How I Started With $300."

She watched it twice.
Then a third time.

The woman in the video didn't have a fancy studio or professional design training. Just a Canva subscription, a laptop, and an Etsy account.

“I can do that,” Nina whispered.

That night, she dug into research. She found that printables—planners, budget sheets, wall art, goal trackers—were booming. Etsy sellers were making hundreds even thousands a month. And with digital products, there was no inventory, no shipping—just passive income.

But to start her shop, Nina would need a few things:

✓ A Canva Pro subscription

✓ Listing photos and mockups

✓ A domain name

✓ Etsy seller fees

✓ A marketing budget for Pinterest and Instagram ads

Total startup cost? Around $750.

She had maybe $150 left after rent and groceries. Her savings account was bleak.

That's when she remembered the **Chase Freedom Flex** card she'd been approved for three months earlier. It was mostly untouched, with a $6,000 limit and 0% APR for 15 months.

She'd been afraid to use it.

Now, she saw it differently—not as a trap, but as **fuel**.

The next morning, she made a promise:
"I'm going to build something that earns while I sleep."

She used $497 of her card limit to pay for everything she needed:

- A year of Canva Pro
- A mini photo shoot with her friend's DSLR camera
- An Etsy Plus subscription
- Tailwind for scheduling Pinterest posts
- A domain name and basic website

Every dollar was tracked in a spreadsheet labeled "Project Nina."

She created her first product—a "30-Day Reset Planner" for overwhelmed moms—and uploaded it to Etsy. Her goal was modest: make $200 in 30 days.

Her first sale came on day six. Then another. Then a $40 bundle order.

By the end of the first month, she had $312 in her PayPal account.

It wasn't just the money. It was the **validation**.

As months passed, Nina released more digital products:

- A homeschool planner for parents
- A wedding checklist printable
- A gratitude journal for teens
- Customizable daily routines

Each new listing cost little but expanded her store. She reinvested a small amount of her income into Pinterest and Instagram ads—and used her card's cashback feature to pay for ad boosts. She was careful never to exceed her budget and made weekly payments toward the balance.

By month five, her Etsy income hit $1,200.
Her card balance? Paid down in full.

That's when she realized:
"I used a credit card to build a business, not debt."

At a family dinner, her cousin asked how she suddenly had time off and a new MacBook.

Nina laughed and said, “You know that card the bank gave me last year? The one I was scared to use? It funded my Etsy shop. I paid it back with profits from printable planners.”

Her uncle, a small business owner, leaned forward. “Wait—so you started a whole business with a credit card and didn’t pay interest?”

“Exactly,” she nodded. “I treated it like an investment, not a shopping spree.”

Today, Nina’s Etsy store brings in over $2,000/month. She spends two hours a week on updates, and most of her income is passive. She’s saving for her first home and teaching other teachers how to monetize their creativity.

She still uses her card—but now, only for things that bring returns.

Because she’s not just a teacher.
She’s a **business owner with a blueprint**—one that started with a decision, a dream, and a little bit of credit.

Chapter 6: Credit Stacking: Unlock $50,000–$100,000 in Interest-Free Capital Without Breaking Your Credit

"Credit stacking is how modern entrepreneurs build fast, grow smart, and fund ideas without asking permission."
— Unknown

What Is Credit Stacking?

Credit stacking is a strategic process of applying for **multiple high-limit credit cards**—both personal and business—in a compressed timeframe to unlock **large amounts of interest-free capital**.

Instead of waiting months or years to build up funding, credit stacking allows you to secure **$50,000 to $100,000 or more** in **under 90 days**.

Why does this work?

Because credit inquiries typically don't show up across all bureaus in real-time, there's a short window—often 24 to 72 hours—where multiple applications can be submitted without the earlier ones negatively impacting the later ones.

Stacking works best when:

- You have good to excellent personal credit (680+)
- You prepare and plan your stack in advance
- You stick to using credit **as a tool**, not a trap

Think of credit stacking as **seeding your business** with zero-interest investment capital. If you treat it seriously, it can change your financial life.

Preparing for the Stack — Clean, Optimize, Strategize

Before stacking, you must prepare your credit profile. Here's how to make sure you're approved for the highest limits possible.

Credit Optimization Checklist:

✓ **Credit Score:** Minimum 700; ideally 720+

✓ **Utilization:** Under 10% across all cards

✓ **Inquiries:** Less than 3 in the last 6 months

✓ **On-Time Payments:** 100% in the past 12 months

✓ **Age of Credit:** At least 1–2 years of credit history

✓ **Credit Mix:** At least 2–3 open accounts (installment + revolving)

Also update your income with current issuers. Your reported income affects limit approvals—even if it's not verified.

Bonus Tip: Remove any outdated or negative accounts from your credit report using tools like Credit Karma or by disputing directly with bureaus.

The 3-Tier Bank Strategy (Apply in This Order)

Different banks have different approval rules. Applying in the right order is **critical** to avoid automatic denials.

Tier 1 – Apply First: Strict Approval Banks

Chase: Follows the 5/24 rule (denied if you've opened 5+ personal cards in 24 months)

US Bank: Conservative approval policy, prefers minimal recent inquiries

Tier 2 – Apply Second: High-Limit Approvers

American Express: Known for generous business lines; won't report business cards to personal credit

Citi: Allows multiple cards if spaced out (8/65/95 rule)

Tier 3 – Apply Last: Easy Approvals or Soft Pull Offers

Capital One: Reports business cards to personal credit—apply last

Navy Federal: Great for high limits if you qualify

Store/Fintech Cards: Apple Card, Petal, or Upgrade—apply only if they're part of your long-term plan

Apply for **3–5 cards in one session**, in the exact order above. Limit yourself to 2–3 personal cards, then move on to 1–3 business cards.

Executing the Stack — Build It, Don't Break It

Once approved, your job isn't done. You need to manage your stack wisely. Log this data as soon as you receive your cards. Set calendar reminders for each due date and promotion expiration.

Use Your Credit for High-Return Investments:

- Launching or scaling a business
- Inventory or equipment for income-generating assets
- Real estate down payments
- Digital ads or brand building
- Coaching, training, or certifications

The rule: **If it doesn't produce income, don't use your stack.**

Avoid These Common Stacking Mistakes

Credit stacking is powerful—but dangerous if used carelessly.

Mistakes to Avoid:

1. **Applying for cards randomly** without planning or bank rules in mind.

2. **Missing payment deadlines**, which can kill 0% APR offers instantly.

3. **Mixing business and personal spending** on the same card.

4. **Carrying balances past the promotional period**—leading to high interest.

5. **Failing to track cards and losing sight of limits, perks, or due dates.**

Remember: You're not using these cards to spend—you're using them to build. Treat every dollar like a seed that must grow.

CREDIT STACKING SUCCESS PLAN (STEP-BY-STEP)

1. **Check your credit** on all three bureaus

2. **Pay down balances** to keep utilization low

3. **Dispute or correct errors** on your report

4. **Plan your stack**: 2–3 personal cards, 2–3 business cards

5. **Apply in one session** following the 3-tier bank strategy

6. **Track every detail** in a spreadsheet

7. **Use cards only for profitable investments**

8. **Set automatic payments** and monitor balances weekly

9. **Pay off or recycle limits** before the 0% period ends

10. **Repeat the stack** in 6–12 months if needed

This is how entrepreneurs use bank capital to build six- and seven-figure businesses—without traditional loans, personal guarantees, or interest.

Real-World Impact:

With smart stacking, you can:

- Fund a business without investors
- Access up to $100K in less than 90 days
- Maintain or even improve your credit score
- Create long-term leverage with short-term action

"Stacking Credit, Stacking Success: How Anthony Unlocked $93,000 in 48 Hours"

Anthony Martinez wasn't broke—he just felt **stuck**.

At 34, he ran a small mobile detailing service in Tampa, Florida. He was good at it. Great, actually. Loyal clients, five-star reviews, a team of two part-time helpers. But every time he tried to expand—buy a van, invest in marketing, upgrade his booking system—he hit the same wall: **no capital**.

Banks weren't lending without a bigger balance sheet. Personal loans came with high interest. His business credit was nonexistent. And the few credit cards he had were small-limit retail cards from his early twenties.

Then, during a late-night YouTube scroll, Anthony heard a word that grabbed his attention:

"Credit stacking."

The video claimed it was possible to get **$50,000 to $100,000 in interest-free capital** without a loan and without hurting your credit—by applying for the right cards, at the right time, in the right order.

Anthony paused the video. Then replayed it. Then took notes.

The next day, he dove headfirst into research. He found blogs, podcasts, even a Reddit group dedicated to credit stacking. He learned that if he optimized his personal credit, applied strategically, and used a mix of personal and **business** credit cards, he could unlock massive funding—without a single loan officer ever saying yes or no.

He spent the next two weeks preparing.

Here's what he did:

- Pulled his credit reports: Experian score was 727
- Paid down two credit cards to drop his utilization below 10%
- Updated his income on existing accounts to reflect recent business growth
- Removed a $45 old phone bill he'd forgotten about

He made a spreadsheet labeled "STACK PLAN" and listed six cards he'd apply for: three personal, three business.

On a Tuesday morning, with a double espresso and nerves kicking in, Anthony launched his plan.

Card 1: *Chase Ink Business Unlimited* – Approved, $20,000
Card 2: *American Express Blue Business Plus* – Approved, $25,000
Card 3: *Citi Custom Cash* – Approved, $12,000
Card 4: *Chase Freedom Unlimited* – Approved, $10,000
Card 5: *Capital One Spark Cash* – Approved, $16,000
Card 6: *Bank of America Cash Rewards* – Approved, $10,000

Total credit approved in less than 48 hours: **$93,000**
All with **0% APR** between 12 to 18 months.

Anthony sat back, stunned.

"I just became my own bank," he whispered.

He didn't go on a shopping spree. He had a blueprint.

He used $6,800 from his new Amex to buy a used commercial van.
$1,200 on branding—logos, business cards, magnetic decals.
$2,300 for a CRM and booking software system.
$4,500 on local Facebook and Google ads.
And $3,000 to hire a virtual assistant for customer service.

He didn't touch the rest.

He created a repayment plan: $800/month toward the balances, starting immediately.

In the next 90 days, his business **doubled**.
He went from 25 clients a week to 60+.
He had so many new bookings that he hired his cousin and gave him a weekly route.
He paid off nearly half his card balances within 4 months.

One weekend, while helping his mom fix her internet, she asked how he was doing.

"I'm great," he said, smiling. "I funded my own business expansion—no loans, no stress."

She looked confused. "How'd you do that?"

"Credit stacking," he said. "I used my good credit and a smart plan to get $90K in capital. Paid zero interest. Built everything faster than I thought possible."

She shook her head. "That's how the rich do it, huh?"

Anthony laughed. "That's how **we** do it now."

Today, Anthony earns three times what he did a year ago.
His credit score? **Still above 740.**
His cards? All current, paid down, and being used strategically.

He's mentoring two friends on how to stack credit for their own businesses. One wants to open a food truck. The other, a mobile pet grooming service.

Because now, Anthony understands:

"You don't need investors. You don't need loans.
You just need to know how to use the system smarter than it was designed for."

Credit stacking didn't just fund his business—it funded his future.

Chapter 7: Rewards Mastery – How to Turn Points, Perks, and Cashback into Wealth and Lifestyle Upgrades

"Most people chase money. The wealthy chase value—and squeeze every dollar for more than it's worth."
— Joe Correa

The Real Value of Credit Card Rewards

When most people think of credit card rewards, they think small: 2% cashback here, 1.5 points per dollar there. But when used strategically, **rewards can save or earn you thousands of dollars per year**—without changing your spending.

There are **three primary types of credit card rewards**:

1. **Cashback** – Direct money back into your pocket

2. **Points** – Flexible reward currencies redeemable for travel, gift cards, or statement credits

3. **Miles** – Airline or hotel-specific rewards, ideal for luxury travel

The key isn't just earning rewards—it's **maximizing their value**. You can earn:

- Free flights worth $1,000+
- Hotel stays that cost $0 out of pocket
- Business class upgrades
- Free insurance, elite status, and lifestyle perks
- Cashback that can fund investments or pay down debt

How to Choose the Right Rewards Strategy for Your Life

Your goals determine your rewards game plan.

Here's how to align your strategy with your lifestyle:

If you want to travel for free:

✓ Focus on **flexible points cards** like:

Chase Sapphire Preferred / Reserve

Amex Gold or Platinum

✓ Transfer points to airline or hotel partners

✓ Book during off-peak dates for maximum value

If you want to earn cash:

✓ Use **flat-rate cashback cards** like:

Citi Double Cash (2%)

Wells Fargo Active Cash

✓ Or rotating category cards like:

Chase Freedom Flex (5% rotating)

Discover It

If you travel for business or with family:

✓ Use cards with perks:

Free checked bags

Priority boarding

Travel insurance

Global Entry/TSA PreCheck reimbursement

Tip: Pick **2–3 core cards** and use them consistently for specific categories: travel, dining, groceries, ads, subscriptions, etc.

How to Redeem Points and Miles for Maximum Value

One of the biggest mistakes people make is redeeming points for **low-value options** like merchandise or low-rate gift cards.

Here's how to **stretch your points for maximum return**:

Best Redemptions (High Value):

- **Transfer to travel partners** (e.g., Hyatt, United, JetBlue)

- **Book through travel portals** with bonus value (Chase Ultimate Rewards adds 25–50%)

- **Upgrade flights or hotels** to business class or suites

Moderate Redemptions (Okay Value):

- **Cashback or statement credits** (usually $0.01 per point)

- **Gift cards** only when discounted

Poor Redemptions (Low Value):

- Shopping on Amazon or with PayPal

- Merchandise via reward portals

- Donating or cashing out below $0.01 per point

Real Example:
50,000 Chase points =
→ $500 in cash
→ $625 in travel (through portal)
→ $900+ when transferred to Hyatt for a 3-night luxury stay

Hidden Perks That Save You Thousands

Beyond points and miles, many credit cards come with **built-in benefits** that most users never claim:

Travel & Purchase Protection

✓ Trip delay/cancellation reimbursement (save $300–$500 per incident)

✓ Lost luggage reimbursement

✓ Rental car insurance

✓ Extended warranty on electronics and appliances

Everyday Use Perks

✓ Cell phone protection (up to $600 if you pay your bill with the card)

✓ Return protection (return denied items)

✓ Purchase protection (covers stolen/damaged items within 90–120 days)

Business Perks

✓ Free employee cards

✓ Spending tracking by category

✓ Discounts through Visa SavingsEdge, Amex Offers, and more

Make a habit of visiting your card's **benefits page** every quarter to remind yourself what's available—and use it.

How to Automate and Multiply Rewards

Once your strategy is in place, **automation** helps you maximize without stress:

Step 1: Set Category Triggers

- Groceries: Use Amex Blue Cash Preferred
- Dining: Use Chase Sapphire
- Gas: Use rotating 5% cards

Step 2: Use Portals to Stack Bonuses

- Use Rakuten, Capital One Shopping, or your card's shopping portal
- Earn up to **10–15% extra cashback** or points

Step 3: Set Up Autopay

- Avoid interest by setting auto-pay to pay in full each month

- Avoid missing out on perks by keeping accounts active

Step 4: Monitor and Reallocate

- Check usage and rewards earned quarterly
- Move low-performing spend to higher-earning cards

Advanced Tip: Pair **multiple cards from the same ecosystem** (e.g., Chase Freedom + Chase Sapphire) to pool points for better redemptions.

Action Plan: Turn Rewards into a Wealth-Boosting System

1. **Pick your goal**: travel, cash, or perks
2. **Select 2–3 main cards** to fit that goal
3. **Assign categories** to each card: food, gas, subscriptions, etc.
4. **Join reward portals** like Rakuten or your issuer's site
5. **Redeem wisely**: Points = travel, cashback = savings or investing

6. **Use perks** to replace insurance or protection you'd otherwise pay for

7. **Review your rewards strategy every 90 days**

Real-World Application

Let's say you spend $2,500/month using three optimized cards. That's $30,000/year. If you average just 3% in combined rewards (points, cash, bonuses), that's **$900–$1,200/year back into your pocket**—with no extra work or spending.

Multiply that over 5 years, and that's $5,000–$6,000 earned passively.
Add in travel redemptions, protections, and card perks? Easily worth **$10,000+.**

"Points for Possibility: How Rachel Traveled the World Without Touching Her Savings"

Rachel Perez didn't travel. Not because she didn't want to—but because, as a single mom and full-time nurse in Dallas, vacations always felt like a luxury she simply couldn't afford.

Her budget was tight. Between rent, daycare, groceries, and student loans, anything left over went into an emergency fund—or didn't go anywhere at all.

So, when her friend Kim invited her on a girls' trip to Puerto Rico, she hesitated.

"I can't drop $1,200 on a vacation," Rachel said.

Kim smiled. "You don't have to. I booked the whole trip using credit card points."

Rachel blinked. "What do you mean? Like miles?"

Kim nodded. "Yup. I haven't paid for a flight in over a year. And I'm not rich—I'm just strategic."

That night, after putting her daughter to bed, Rachel stayed up late reading everything she could about credit card rewards. By 1:30 a.m., she had opened four browser tabs, downloaded three PDFs, and had a notebook full of scribbled phrases like "transfer partners," "5/24 rule," and "travel portals."

She couldn't believe what she had discovered.

Over the next week, Rachel built her first credit rewards plan.

She applied for the **Chase Sapphire Preferred** card, was approved for $9,000, and earned **60,000 bonus points** after meeting the spending requirement over the next three months—on things she already paid for: daycare, groceries, and gas.

Then she paired it with the **Chase Freedom Flex**, which offered 5% rotating categories and another bonus.

She spent intentionally, tracked her rewards, and watched her points grow.

Three months later, she logged into the Chase travel portal and found **roundtrip flights to Puerto Rico for 22,000 points** and a **4-night beachfront hotel for 34,000 points**.

Out-of-pocket cost?
$67 total in taxes and fees.

Rachel cried when she hit "book now."

The trip wasn't just a getaway—it was a life-changer.

She walked barefoot on white sand beaches, drank coffee on a balcony overlooking the ocean, and danced with strangers under the stars. For once, she didn't feel like she was scraping by—she felt free.

When she got home, she doubled down.

She opened an **American Express Gold Card**, this time focusing on dining rewards and grocery spend. She added **Rakuten**, **Southwest Rapid Rewards Dining**, and a few shopping portals to her arsenal.

Soon, every dollar she spent—on school supplies, gas, food—was earning her something back. But she never spent more than she planned. She paid in full. Every. Single. Month.

Over the next 18 months, Rachel used rewards to:

- Visit her sister in Chicago (flights covered with points)
- Take her daughter to Disney World (hotel 100% booked with points)
- Fly to Denver for a nursing conference (paid for with a sign-up bonus)
- Stay in a 4-star hotel in New York for a weekend girls' trip—completely on points

She even used cashback to cover unexpected car repairs and Amazon gift cards to help with holiday shopping.

One afternoon, while helping her daughter with homework, Rachel smiled as she checked her rewards balance:
112,000 points, $147 in cashback, two free hotel nights pending.

She wasn't just earning back money. She was building **a new lifestyle.**

At her next nursing staff meeting, her coworkers joked about needing a break.

Rachel pulled out her phone and said, "You know you can fly roundtrip to San Diego for 12,000 points and stay at the Hyatt downtown for free, right?"

They looked at her like she had just revealed a magic trick.

One of them whispered, “Rachel... you travel more than anyone I know. How do you afford all that?”

She replied with a smile, “Points. I make my money work twice.”

Today, Rachel is still a full-time nurse. Still a single mom. But she’s also a **travel hacker**, a rewards strategist, and a low-key credit card expert among her friends.

She pays zero interest. Carries no debt. And treats every purchase like an investment—because it is.

“It’s not about spending more,” she says. “It’s about getting more from what I already spend.”

And what started as a reluctant “no” to a Puerto Rico trip turned into a five-country travel streak—powered entirely by rewards, discipline, and knowledge.

Chapter 8: Wealth Cycling: How to Rotate, Reinvest, and Grow Using Credit Rewards, Cashback, and Credit Lines

"The secret to long-term financial success isn't making one big move—it's cycling small, smart moves over and over."
— Joe Correa

What Is Wealth Cycling?

Wealth cycling is the process of using credit cards, rewards, cashback, and 0% APR opportunities in a continuous loop to:

✓ Access capital

✓ Fund income-generating activities

✓ Redeem rewards or profits

✓ Pay back credit

✓ Repeat—on a higher level

This is how people build wealth without loans, venture capital, or massive savings. It's a system that reinvests itself. When done correctly, wealth cycling becomes **a reliable rhythm of building and scaling** using tools you already have.

The 5-Part Wealth Cycling Formula

Let's break down the core cycle step by step:

Step 1: Fund with Credit

Use 0% APR cards or available credit lines to:

- Start or scale a business
- Run an ad campaign
- Purchase high-demand inventory
- Pay for a course or mentorship

Use only **intentional credit**—not emotional spending.

Step 2: Build Income or Asset Value

Convert the borrowed capital into something productive:

- A digital product that sells passively

- A flipping hustle that returns profit
- Rental setup or service equipment

Track every dollar. Know what your capital is earning.

Step 3: Reap Rewards or Revenue

As income rolls in or rewards build up:

- Redeem points for travel or cashback
- Collect payments from clients
- Receive affiliate, ad, or platform payouts

This is where cash flow or value is realized.

Step 4: Pay Down Card & Recycle Limit

Start paying back the credit card(s) used:

- Set auto-pay for minimums
- Aggressively pay down principal with profit
- Free up available credit for the next round

As you reduce debt and maintain payment history, your score increases and your limits rise.

Step 5: Repeat at a Higher Level

Now that your cards are paid down, rewards earned, and profits made—do it again:

- Apply for another 0% APR offer
- Invest in a larger project
- Stack multiple cards
- Redeem bigger bonuses

Each cycle builds more momentum than the last.

Real-World Wealth Cycling Examples

Let's see this in action:

Example 1 – Digital Course Launch

1. Use $2,500 from a 0% APR card to build a course (camera, hosting, software)
2. Launch the course and earn $6,000 over 6 months
3. Pay off the card with $3,000, keeping $3,000 profit
4. Points earned = 2,500+ (used for free travel)

5. Repeat with upgraded materials or a second course

Example 2 – Inventory Flipping

1. Spend $4,000 on liquidation pallets or sneaker resale

2. Flip items for $7,000 in revenue

3. Pay off card, keep $3,000+ profit

4. Cashback: 2% = $80 bonus

5. Reinvest into larger or multiple orders

Example 3 – Service Business Scaling

1. Use $3,000 to set up website, branding, and ads for a cleaning business

2. Secure $1,200/month in recurring contracts

3. Break even in 90 days, then use cash flow to expand

4. Points from ad spend used for a hotel stay or cashback to fund insurance

5. Repeat for another local service niche

Tools to Automate and Track Wealth Cycles

Smart cycling requires smart tracking. Use these tools:

Spreadsheets:

✓ Create a master "cycle dashboard"

✓ Track spend, repayment dates, ROI, rewards earned

Apps:

- **Credit Karma / Experian:** Monitor score & utilization
- **Mint or Monarch Money:** Track spend by card
- **AwardWallet or CardPointers:** Manage card benefits & expirations
- **Google Calendar:** Set reminders for due dates and 0% expiration periods

Journaling:

Keep a simple "Wealth Log" where you record:

What you used credit for

What came of it

What you learned

What to do next cycle

Pitfalls to Avoid When Cycling Credit for Wealth

Wealth cycling is powerful—but only with **discipline**.

Avoid these common traps:

✘ **Spending for lifestyle, not leverage**

✘ **Missing minimum payments** (which cancels 0% offers)

✘ **Overestimating profits before they're earned**

✘ **Not tracking results, leading to waste**

✘ **Mixing business and personal transactions blindly**

Stay focused. This is a strategy, not a shortcut.

ACTION PLAN TO BEGIN WEALTH CYCLING TODAY

Here's how to get started:

1. **Review your credit limits and 0% offers**—what capital is currently available?

2. **Decide on one income-producing use**: course, resale, content, service, etc.

3. **Create a simple plan**: total cost, ROI goal, timeframe

4. **Use credit to fund only that plan**, nothing else

5. **Track your results and payments weekly**

6. **Set a "cycle close date"** (when your goal ends and credit is repaid)

7. **Assess results, redeem rewards**, and begin again

Final Thought

"Wealth is built in cycles. The faster and smarter you cycle, the faster you grow."

Credit doesn't just buy time—it buys possibility. When you use it wisely and repeat your success rhythm, you're no longer playing defense with money.

You're building offense—with every swipe.

"The Cycle That Built a Business: How Eli Turned Credit Into Compounding Wealth"

Eli Washington didn't look like someone who used credit cards to build wealth. He didn't wear expensive clothes or drive a flashy car. Most days, he wore a hoodie, jeans, and sneakers worn thin from walking.

But ask anyone in his Atlanta neighborhood, and they'd tell you: Eli had one of the most quietly successful landscaping businesses around. He didn't come from money. He didn't have investors. And he sure didn't take out a loan from the bank.

Instead, Eli built his business with something most people overlook: **a simple credit card.**

It started three years ago.

He was tired of living paycheck to paycheck working at a warehouse, always watching other people win. One night, scrolling through Instagram, he came across a story: a woman who launched a six-figure business using **a 0% APR credit card**.

"Build first, pay later," she said. "Credit is capital—if you respect it."

That sentence stuck in his head.

Eli pulled his credit report. His score was 702—not bad. He'd never missed a payment, but he'd also never used credit to do anything meaningful.

He applied for a **Wells Fargo Reflect Card**—18 months 0% APR on purchases. Approved for $7,500.

He stared at the screen for 10 minutes, realizing what just happened.

"This is it," he whispered. "Seed money."

Eli didn't blow the limit. He had a plan:

1. Buy second-hand landscaping equipment
2. Register his LLC and get business cards printed
3. Build a basic website and run $200 in local Facebook ads
4. Offer neighbors a discounted service to build testimonials

He used $3,200 of the card. Then set up auto-pay for $200 a month, knowing he had 18 months to pay it off interest-free.

Within 60 days, he had 14 paying clients.

By month three, he'd brought in $4,000 in revenue and already made two early payments toward the card balance. But he wasn't done.

Eli started what he later called his **"wealth cycle."**

As money came in, he paid off the card and **reused the available credit** for growth:

☑ He reinvested in better tools

☑ Bought branded uniforms

☑ Launched a referral rewards program

Every dollar borrowed had a purpose. Every payment had a plan.

Once that card was 80% paid off, he applied for a **Chase Ink Business Unlimited** card and got approved for $20,000—at 0% APR for 12 months.

This time, he used it to:

- Hire part-time help
- Add gutter cleaning and pressure washing to his services
- Pay for SEO and Google Ads

His income doubled.

By the end of year one, Eli had:

✓ Paid off his first credit card in full

✓ Used two cards to rotate funds and scale faster

✓ Built a client base of 80+ homes

✓ Maintained a personal credit score of 735

✓ Traveled to Miami on points for a much-needed break

✓ Saved over $1,200 using cashback and rewards

One night, sitting on his porch with his cousin Marcus, Eli explained his system.

"I just keep cycling," he said. "I borrow, I build, I earn, I repay—and then I repeat. I don't take on debt. I use credit as a temporary tool to level up. No interest. No pressure."

Marcus asked, "But don't you get stressed borrowing like that?"

Eli shook his head. "Not when you've got a plan and the income to back it. It's not about debt—it's about **discipline**."

Today, Eli runs a six-figure landscaping and property maintenance business with four part-time employees. His personal and business credit are both strong. He teaches workshops on how to responsibly use credit to scale small businesses.

He still tracks every card in a spreadsheet. He still sets calendar alerts for payment due dates and 0% promo expirations. And he still follows the same cycle:

1. Fund a goal
2. Grow with intention
3. Collect and reinvest
4. Pay down and prepare for the next level

He calls it **"rotating responsibility."**

"Most people see credit as a trap," he says. "But if you build with it—if you respect it—it becomes the most consistent investor you'll ever have."

And it all started with a $7,500 card... and a belief that credit could be something more.

Chapter 9: Business Credit Mastery – Build Business Credit Fast and Separate It from Your Personal Profile

"Personal credit gets you started. Business credit scales you—quietly, powerfully, and without personal risk."
— Joe Correa

Why Business Credit Matters

Most people run their businesses on **personal credit cards**, personal loans, or their own savings. But the truly scalable path to wealth?
It's **business credit.**

When you build business credit the right way, you can:

✓ Access higher credit limits

✓ Protect your personal credit score

✓ Qualify for funding regardless of personal income

✓ Secure 0% APR business cards that don't report to personal bureaus

✓ Position your company for loans, lines of credit, equipment financing, and vendor terms

The key is **separating your personal identity from your business profile**—while using your good credit to get the ball rolling.

How Business Credit Works (and Why It's Different)

Business credit has its **own ecosystem**, built on these core principles:

1. **EIN (Employer Identification Number)** – Your business's SSN

2. **Business credit bureaus** – Experian Business, Equifax Business, Dun & Bradstreet

3. **Trade lines (vendor accounts)** – Establish payment history and creditworthiness

4. **Paydex Score (D&B)** – A 0–100 score based on how fast your business pays its bills

Unlike personal credit, business credit:

- Doesn't require a social security number to build

- Can be grown much faster (in 3–6 months)
- Isn't tied to your personal utilization or inquiries

And the best part? Some business cards (like those from Amex, Chase, and Capital One) **don't report to your personal credit**—even if you carry a balance.

STEP-BY-STEP PLAN TO BUILD BUSINESS CREDIT FROM SCRATCH

Step 1: Set Up Your Business Properly

Lenders want to see that your business is **legit** and established.

➔ Register your business as an **LLC or Corporation**

➔ Get an **EIN** from the IRS (free)

➔ Open a **business checking account**

➔ Get a **professional phone number and business address** (even virtual)

➔ List your business with **411 Directory Assistance**

Make sure your business name, phone, and address match **exactly** across all documents and websites.

Step 2: Open 3–5 Net 30 Vendor Accounts

These vendors extend credit to your business and report payment history to business credit bureaus. You buy products and pay **within 30 days** (Net 30 terms).

Recommended starter vendors:

Uline (office and shipping supplies)

Grainger (tools and hardware)

Summa Office Supplies

Nav (business credit monitoring)

Crown Office Supplies

Place small orders (e.g., $50–100), pay early, and let them report to D&B or Experian.

Step 3: Get Your D-U-N-S Number

This is your **Dun & Bradstreet ID**. Required to build a Paydex score.

- Go to dnb.com and apply for your D-U-N-S number (free for business credit building)

- Use your exact business information

- Link your Net 30 accounts to your DUNS once they start reporting

After 2–3 on-time payments, your **Paydex score** will begin to form. Aim for 80 or higher.

Step 4: Apply for Business Credit Cards

After you've opened 3–5 vendor accounts and used them responsibly for 60–90 days, you're ready to apply for **true revolving business credit.**

Recommended business credit cards:

- ➢ **Chase Ink Business Unlimited** – High limit, 0% APR, no annual fee

- ➢ **Amex Blue Business Plus** – 2x points on all purchases

- ➢ **Capital One Spark Cash** – Great for cashback

- ➢ **Divvy or Brex** – Fintech cards with flexible underwriting

Use your EIN and business info. Some may ask for your SSN for a **personal guarantee**—this is fine during the early stages.

Bonus: Many business cards don't show up on your personal report, even if approved using your SSN.

How to Use Business Credit Without Hurting Personal Credit

Here's how you keep personal credit clean and business credit growing:

Use Business Cards Exclusively for Business

✓ Separate business and personal expenses

✓ Don't mix grocery or gas purchases with your business ad spend

Avoid Maxing Out Business Cards

✓ Keep usage under 50% unless it's temporary

✓ Business utilization isn't scored the same—but lenders still see it

Pay Vendors and Creditors Early

- Paying Net 30 vendors 10–15 days early boosts your Paydex score

- Auto-pay your minimums to avoid late payments

Track Your Credit Separately

- Use **Nav** to monitor your business scores

- Use your personal apps (e.g., Credit Karma) for your FICO and utilization

Business Credit Expansion Plan (for 6–12 Months)

Month 1–2:

- Form LLC, get EIN, open business bank account

- Apply for 3 Net 30 accounts and make small purchases

- Get a D-U-N-S number

Month 3–4:

- Add 2 more vendor accounts

- Begin monitoring your business credit on Nav

- Ensure payment history is being reported

Month 5–6:

- Apply for 1–2 business credit cards
- Use cards only for business expenses
- Begin rotating rewards and building credit lines

Month 7–12:

- Apply for higher-tier business cards or lines of credit
- Leverage rewards or 0% APR for business growth
- Pay off balances with business revenue
- Separate personal credit from operations

By month 12, you'll be positioned to:

- Apply for larger credit limits
- Qualify for SBA funding, equipment leases, or real estate

- Scale your company without touching personal resources

Final Thought

"You can hustle your way to a few thousand. But if you want to scale, you need structure—and credit gives you that structure."

Business credit is not just a tool—it's a shield. It protects your personal profile, expands your funding options, and gives your business the identity it needs to grow.

Start small. Build smart. And let your business earn the right to grow—without dragging your personal credit down with it.

"The Invisible Ladder: How Darnell Built Business Credit and Stopped Risking His Personal Score"

Darnell Hayes had ambition. What he didn't have—yet—was capital.

He ran a small media business out of his garage in Charlotte, North Carolina. He filmed promotional videos for barbershops, fitness trainers, and real estate agents. He was talented, hungry, and resourceful.

But his biggest problem? Every time he upgraded his gear or ran a Facebook ad campaign, he put it on his **personal credit cards**.

The result?

A personal credit score that hovered in the low 600s, nearly maxed-out cards, and zero room to grow.

"I'm building a business," he told himself. But what he was really doing... was burying his own financial foundation.

Then one day, while filming a podcast interview for a startup founder, something clicked.

The guest said, "I never use my personal credit for business. I built everything using business credit—separate cards, separate lines, even a DUNS number."

Darnell paused mid-recording. "Wait... what's a DUNS number?"

The guest laughed. "It's like a credit score for your business. And once you build it, you don't have to touch your personal profile again."

After the session, Darnell stayed up past midnight watching YouTube videos and reading blog posts. The next morning, he printed a checklist titled:

"How to Build Business Credit Without Using Personal Credit."

Step one? **Form an LLC.**

He'd been operating as a sole proprietor for two years. It was easy, but it had no credibility. Within a week, he filed his LLC papers for “Hayes Media Co.” and applied for an EIN with the IRS.

Step two? **Get a business checking account.**

He walked into his credit union, opened the account, and deposited $1,000 he’d been saving for a new drone. From now on, every dollar earned by Hayes Media would go through this account.

Step three? **Set up Net 30 vendor accounts.**

He signed up with Uline and Grainger—vendors that let him buy supplies now and pay within 30 days. He ordered a few things he needed anyway: gloves, extension cords, portable lighting kits. Then he paid early.

He added two more vendors: Summa Office Supplies and Nav, which also let him track his new business credit profile.

A few weeks later, he got an email from Dun & Bradstreet:
Your D-U-N-S Number Has Been Created.

That same day, he checked Nav again—**his business Paydex score was now live.**

He had officially entered the world of business credit.

Two months later, with three vendor accounts reporting and his LLC showing consistent deposits, he applied for the **Chase Ink Business Unlimited** card.

Approved. $15,000 limit. 0% APR for 12 months.
And best of all? **It didn't show up on his personal credit report.**

He used it to upgrade his editing laptop and prepay ad campaigns. He paid it back in chunks, using client payments that came in weekly.

A month later, he applied for the **Amex Blue Business Plus** card. Approved again—$20,000 limit.

His confidence soared.

One weekend, at a BBQ with his cousins, they started talking money.

"You still putting all that business stuff on your own credit cards?" one asked.

Darnell shook his head. "Nope. I've got three business cards now. None of them touch my personal report."

His cousin frowned. "How'd you do that?"

"I stopped acting like a freelancer. I built a real business. I've got an LLC, an EIN, and a DUNS number. Now the banks lend to my *business*, not me."

They looked at him like he had just cracked the cheat code. And he had.

Because for the first time ever, Darnell had:

✓ $50,000 in business credit access

✓ A 90-day buffer to grow before paying interest

✓ A healthy personal credit score again

✓ A system to separate his business from his name

Today, Hayes Media is no longer just a side hustle—it's a growing brand.

Darnell uses business cards to travel to film conferences, book last-minute rentals, and run split-test ads for clients. He's hired an intern. He's bidding on larger contracts.

And most importantly, his personal credit is clean. Protected. Safe.

"I used to feel like I was growing my business on quicksand," he says. "Now? I've got a foundation."

And it all started with a checklist, a late-night research binge... and a decision to treat his business like one.

Chapter 10: The Lifetime Credit Strategy: How to Maintain, Multiply, and Pass On Credit Wealth

"Credit mastery isn't a one-time win—it's a lifelong strategy that creates stability, freedom, and legacy."
— Joe Correa

The Big Picture – Why Credit Is a Long-Term Game

You've now learned how to:

☑ Build and protect personal credit

☑ Stack credit for capital and business

☑ Use 0% APR and high limits strategically

☑ Earn and multiply rewards

☑ Build business credit separate from your personal profile

Create wealth cycles that reinvest and grow

Now, in this final chapter, we shift focus from tactics to longevity.

This is your **lifetime credit strategy**—a practical plan for:

- Maintaining elite credit
- Repeating growth without risk
- Preparing for high-level funding
- Protecting your financial identity
- Teaching the next generation

Build, Rotate, and Rest

The most successful credit users rotate through 3 phases every year:

Phase 1: Build

✓ Apply for 1–2 new cards (business or personal) with strong rewards or 0% offers

✓ Increase credit limits with existing cards

✓ Open new trade lines for your business

✓ Set up automation tools (autopay, trackers, calendar alerts)

Phase 2: Rotate

✓ Use credit to fund profitable activity (business launch, ad campaign, travel, equipment)

✓ Earn rewards and cashback

✓ Pay back balances systematically

✓ Monitor score weekly for changes

Phase 3: Rest and Reflect

✓ Stop applying for new credit for 3–6 months

✓ Focus on increasing income and savings

✓ Audit your reward redemptions and ROI

✓ Decide what worked and what didn't before the next build cycle

This cycle creates **rhythm without pressure**—and allows your credit to grow predictably over time.

Protecting Your Credit and Financial Identity

As your credit access grows, **so does your exposure**. Here's how to protect yourself:

Credit Protection Tools

- Freeze your credit reports when not applying (Equifax, Experian, TransUnion)
- Use identity theft protection apps like **Aura**, **LifeLock**, or **Credit Karma**
- Set **2FA (two-factor authentication)** on every financial account
- Use different, strong passwords for each bank and credit app

Smart Monitoring Habits

✓ Check reports every 30 days

✓ Dispute incorrect items immediately

✓ Get notifications for new accounts or credit pulls

✓ Track your credit utilization by individual card

Remember: One stolen identity or one reporting error can wipe out years of good standing if you're not monitoring.

Advanced Credit Moves as You Grow

As your income and business expand, you'll want to level up your credit strategy:

Set Up a Holding Company

- Use an LLC or Corporation to hold properties, digital assets, or brands

- Apply for credit under that entity once it builds business credit

Establish Banking Relationships

➔ Open accounts with local and regional banks

➔ Build trust with business bankers and ask about:

◆ Business lines of credit

◆ Equipment or fleet financing

◆ Real estate or investment lending

Leverage Personal and Business Credit Together

✓ Use 0% APR business cards for working capital

✓ Use personal rewards cards for high-category spend (groceries, travel)

✓ Use cashback to fund tax payments or reinvest into new ventures

Pro Tip: Credit is just the first layer. With good credit and business history, you unlock **private funding, real estate leverage, and strategic capital partnerships.**

Building Credit Legacy

Credit mastery isn't just for you—it's something you can pass on.

Teach Your Kids or Family

➔ Add a child as an **authorized user** on a card (age 13+ for many banks)

➔ Help them build a score before they even turn 18

➔ Teach them to pay in full and use rewards wisely

➔ Show them how business credit works and how to build it early

Share With Your Community

➔ Host a credit education night for your church, school, or group

➔ Create a workbook or checklist based on your journey

➔ Help others rise without judgment

This multiplies your impact and turns what you've learned into **generational wisdom**.

Lifetime Credit Success Plan (Use Annually)

1. **Review** personal and business credit reports quarterly

2. **Apply** for 1–2 strategic cards each year with purpose

3. **Rotate** spending and rewards based on current business goals

4. **Use** credit for building assets, never lifestyle inflation

5. **Redeem** points or cashback efficiently

6. **Pay off** high balances before promotional periods end

7. **Teach** at least one person per year what you've learned

Over a decade, this system adds up to:

- Hundreds of thousands in accessible capital
- Tens of thousands in saved interest
- Five- or six-figure value in points, perks, and cashback
- A legacy of knowledge and smart credit behavior

Final Thought

“Credit doesn’t just buy you what you want—it unlocks who you can become.”

You now hold the tools that most people never take the time to learn. With discipline, intention, and strategic rotation, you can turn credit into income, rewards into wealth, and knowledge into legacy.

This is not the end. It’s the beginning of a lifetime of financial control.

Go build something great—with the credit you now command.

“Legacy in Motion: How One Man Turned Credit Mastery Into Generational Wealth”

Marcus Fulton never considered himself a “money guy.” He worked hard, paid his bills on time, and made sure his kids had what they needed. He wasn’t flashy—just focused.

But in his early 40s, after back-to-back layoffs and rising credit card debt, he realized something chilling:

“I’m not building anything they can inherit.”

He meant his children. His wife, Denise, reassured him. “We’ve always gotten by,” she said.

But Marcus didn’t want to “get by” anymore. He wanted to leave behind more than stories—he wanted to leave behind structure.

It started with a podcast episode he listened to on a late-night drive home. The guest was a retired entrepreneur who said:

"The first time I felt wealthy wasn't when I made six figures—it was when I had $150,000 in available credit and zero balances. That's when I could breathe."

That sentence flipped a switch.

Marcus had never thought of credit that way. He always saw it as a trap. Something to be feared, not leveraged. But that night, he made a commitment:

He would **learn everything about credit**. Not just how to fix his score, but how to use it—for cash flow, rewards, growth, and eventually, legacy.

He started simply: pulling his credit report and watching YouTube videos after the kids went to bed.

What he found shocked him.

He'd been carrying a 665 score for years, all because of high utilization on two cards and an old medical collection he didn't even know about. He paid off balances strategically, disputed the error, and within three months, his score was 734.

He felt powerful.

He then applied for his first **0% APR card** with Chase. Approved. $11,500 limit. He used it to pay off a high-interest balance from another card and immediately began planning a rotation strategy.

By year's end, he had:

- Three personal cards with over $40,000 in available credit
- Paid $0 in interest
- Collected over 78,000 points—used to take the kids to Disney for the first time

But he didn't stop there.

In year two, Marcus launched a side business with his son: **a vending machine company**.

They formed an LLC, got an EIN, and opened a business checking account. He used vendor accounts to start building business credit. Then, applied for the **Amex Blue Business Cash** card.

Approved. $20,000 limit.

The vending machines turned $2,000 in startup costs into $7,800 in the first year—and every cent earned ran through their business credit profile.

His son, just 17 at the time, was added as an **authorized user** on one of Marcus's oldest cards. By the time he turned 18, he had a credit score of 765.

Marcus smiled every time he saw it.

"My son started life with what I didn't have until I was 45."

By year three, Marcus had a system:

- ➔ One personal card for groceries and gas
- ➔ One travel card for family trips
- ➔ One business card for expenses
- ➔ Cashback was reinvested into a stock portfolio
- ➔ Points paid for flights and hotels
- ➔ A digital tracker with all payment due dates and APR periods
- ➔ Biweekly credit check reminders
- ➔ Annual credit "audits" in January and July

He even hosted a family meeting once a year to review credit goals—like most families would plan a vacation.

Denise started calling it **"the Fulton Family Credit Summit."**

The real reward came the day his daughter came home from college orientation and said, “Dad, my roommate just maxed out her card buying a TV. I told her about how we rotate spending and pay in full every time.”

Marcus laughed. “You teaching the class now?”

“No,” she said, “just paying the knowledge forward.”

He walked away quietly, tears forming.

Because it wasn’t about the score. Or the credit lines. Or the travel perks.

It was about **changing the default**—so that his children would never again see credit as survival. They would see it as a strategy. A tool. A launchpad.

Today, Marcus teaches financial literacy at a local youth center. He helps young adults understand credit, build responsibly, and avoid common traps.

His legacy isn’t a mansion or a massive inheritance.

It’s something stronger:
A working system they can use. A mindset they can trust. A future they can fund—one swipe, one cycle, one decision at a time.

“I may not leave behind millions,” he says, “but I left behind the map.”

And for his family, that map is worth more than gold.

Final Words from the Author

"From Surviving to Strategizing: Why This Is Just the Beginning"

There's something powerful about closing a book—not because the story ends, but because your story begins.

If you've made it this far, I want to say something that you may not hear often:

I'm proud of you.

This isn't just a credit book. It's a manual for rewiring how we think about money, opportunity, and control. And the fact that you stayed with me through every chapter means you're not like most people. You're ready for something greater.

The Day I Took Credit Seriously

I still remember the day I decided to stop being afraid of credit. I had just been denied for a simple $1,000 personal loan—even though I had a decent job, a stable home, and big dreams.

The bank didn't care. The numbers didn't add up.

That was my wake-up call. I realized that in this system, **credit wasn't about who you are—it was about what you understand.**

From that point on, I made it my mission to understand every part of how credit works:

➔ How to raise your score without going broke

➔ How to rotate cards without hurting your report

➔ How to use credit cards to fund your business, your goals, even your lifestyle

➔ How to protect yourself and teach your kids what schools never will

Everything I learned, I poured into this book.

Because I don't want anyone to feel that kind of rejection again—not you, not your family, not your kids.

Why Credit Is More Than Numbers

It's easy to think of credit as just scores, interest rates, or approval odds.

But I've learned that credit is really about **choices**.

When you have good credit:

- You choose when to borrow, not beg

- You choose where to live, not just what's available

- You choose how to grow your business, not whether you can afford to

- You choose freedom, not fear

Bad credit feels like being stuck. Good credit feels like breathing again.

And when you combine **good credit** with **a good plan**, that's where wealth begins.

What I Hope You Take From This

If you only remember three things from this entire series, let them be these:

1. **Credit is a tool, not a trap.**
When you respect it, it gives you leverage. When you ignore it, it punishes you. But it's never your enemy—it's a system waiting to be mastered.

2. **Use credit to build, not to buy time.**
Every dollar borrowed should either return more money, save you time, or create a long-term benefit. If it doesn't? Reconsider the swipe.

3. **Your legacy is in the habits you teach.**
Whether you're a parent, a mentor, or just someone who wants to break the cycle—remember: someone is always watching. If you build right, others will follow. You're not just improving your credit. You're changing your financial DNA.

What's Next on Your Journey

This book isn't the end—it's your new beginning. So what should you do next?

Here's a quick roadmap I recommend:

Audit Your Current Credit – Know your scores, reports, balances, APRs, due dates

Set a Credit Rotation Plan – Create a 12-month strategy: earn, redeem, repay

Leverage 0% APR Offers – Only for wealth-building actions: business, education, investing in yourself

Build Business Credit – Create a structure where your name doesn't carry all the risk

Start Teaching – Help someone else (even one person) understand what you just learned

And if you're not sure how to do that, I've created more books, courses, and tools that walk you through each step. You can find those in the *Credit to Capital* series or visit my official site for free resources.

A Personal Message for You

I wrote this book for the underdog.
For the person who didn't grow up learning about credit.
For the single mom trying to rebuild.
For the immigrant learning a new system.
For the hustler who's tired of the hustle.
For the dreamer who got denied—and still dreams anyway.

I see you.

If I could sit across from you, look you in the eyes, and say one thing, it would be this:

You are not behind. You're right on time.

Start where you are. Use what you have. Learn what you need.

Credit is a game—and now you've got the rulebook. So go play to win. Build boldly. Borrow wisely. Teach freely.

And never, ever forget: **You are your best investment.**

Epilogue

"The Credit Compass – A New Direction for Life, Wealth, and Freedom": The Journey You Just Took

You've done something that most people never will.

You didn't just fix your credit—you redefined how you approach it.

Most people either ignore credit or fear it. You chose to **face it, study it, and master it.** That means something. It means you're ready for the next level—not just in your finances, but in your entire life.

This journey we've taken together wasn't about chasing a higher score or collecting a few points. It was about something much deeper:

- Learning how the credit system works
- Using it as a lever for opportunity
- Protecting your financial foundation
- Building income, assets, and confidence
- Passing on a mindset of control, not confusion

And now, you're no longer wandering in the dark—you have a **credit compass**.

You know which direction to go.

Your Life, Now with Leverage

Imagine this...

You walk into a bank to apply for a line of credit—not because you're desperate, but because you have a plan. You know your score, your credit history, your limits. You already have vendor accounts, 0% APR cards, and a business bank account with consistent cash flow.

You're not applying with your hat in your hand—you're negotiating from a position of power.

That's what **real leverage** looks like.

And once you taste that feeling, you'll never go back to surviving. You'll be building, strategizing, and multiplying your success year after year.

"Credit isn't about what you can buy today—it's about what you can build forever."

The Ripple Effect of Responsibility

One of the most important realizations about credit is that **your actions ripple outward**.

When you take control of your credit:

➔ Your family sees it

➔ Your coworkers feel it

➔ Your community benefits from it

➔ Your future self thanks you for it

Every late payment you avoid, every balance you pay off, every smart card rotation you execute—it all adds up. It becomes a model others can follow. It becomes legacy.

So I challenge you to be **the first in your circle** to:

- Build a perfect credit rotation system
- Maximize rewards and cashback
- Create a business credit profile from scratch
- Educate your kids, spouse, or siblings on how credit really works

Because when you lead by example, **others rise with you**.

Other Books in the *Credit to Capital* Series

By Joe Correa

Unlock the full financial journey with these powerful and practical books in the *Credit to Capital* series. Each volume is designed to help you build, repair, and leverage credit to create wealth, purchase property, and launch businesses—no matter where you're starting from.

- **Book 1: How to Establish Credit in the U.S.**
- **Book 2: Personal Credit Repair Blueprint**
- **Book 3: How to Build Credit Fast Without Debt**
- **Book 4: Business Credit Mastery**
- **Book 5: Credit Card Secrets for Building Wealth & Rewards**
- **Book 6: Credit Card Hacking for Smart Borrowers**
- **Book 7: How to Leverage Business Credit to Fund Real Estate Purchases**
- **Book 8: Business Credit Ecosystem: Build, Stack & Automate Unlimited Funding Without Personal Risk**
- **Book 9: How to Get $1M in Credit and Keep It**
- **Book 10: Credit-Funded Wealth for Families**

www.ingramcontent.com/pod-product-compliance
Ingram Content Group UK Ltd.
Pitfield, Milton Keynes, MK11 3LW, UK
UKHW020158290926
15471UKWH00005B/946

9 798349 609473